Sports Build Character

COURAGE IN SPORTS

by Todd Kortemeier

FOCUS READERS

FOCUS READERS

www.focusreaders.com

Focus Readers is distributed by North Star Editions:
sales@northstareditions.com | 888-417-0195

Produced for Focus Readers by Red Line Editorial.

Photographs ©: technotr/iStockphoto, cover, 1; nycshooter/iStockphoto, 4–5, 29; asiseeit/iStockphoto, 7; AP Images, 8–9; HH/AP Images, 11; Erin Combs/Toronto Star/Getty Images, 12; cnicbc/iStockphoto, 15; Susan Ragan/AP Images, 16; John Gaps III/AP Images, 19; Shuji Kajiyama/AP Images, 20; imgorthand/iStockphoto, 22–23; Wavebreakmedia/iStockphoto, 25; martinedoucet/iStockphoto, 26–27

ISBN
978-1-63517-531-8 (hardcover)
978-1-63517-603-2 (paperback)
978-1-63517-747-3 (ebook pdf)
978-1-63517-675-9 (hosted ebook)

Library of Congress Control Number: 2017948112

Printed in the United States of America
Mankato, MN
November, 2017

About the Author

Todd Kortemeier is a writer and editor from Minneapolis. He has written more than 50 books for young people, primarily on sports topics.

TABLE OF CONTENTS

CHAPTER 1

WHAT IS COURAGE?

Everyone is afraid sometimes. Athletes are no different. Fear is a part of competing.

Sports involve many obstacles. An athlete's job is to overcome them. Courage means facing fears.

Gymnasts show courage by trying new moves.

It means taking on tough situations. And it means believing in success.

Courage on the field can take many forms. It may mean pushing through an injury to finish the job. It can also involve standing up for what is right.

Having courage in sports can also have an impact off the field. Courage is about knowing right

LET'S DISCUSS

When are times that you need courage?

It takes courage to stand up after an injury.

from wrong. Having courage is not always easy. But it is necessary when times get tough.

CHAPTER 2

COURAGE IN ACTION

Jackie Robinson showed courage every time he walked onto the baseball field. Many fans didn't want him there. Even some of his teammates didn't want him. It was because he was black.

Jackie Robinson won the Rookie of the Year Award in 1947.

Robinson joined the Brooklyn Dodgers in 1947. For years, black players were not allowed in Major League Baseball (MLB). Robinson broke through the color barrier. He faced a lot of **discrimination**. Fans often yelled **insults**.

Off the field, Robinson was barely a part of the team. He had to stay in

LET'S DISCUSS

Would fans have needed courage to cheer for Jackie Robinson in 1947? Why or why not?

Robinson sits beside the other infielders at his first major league game.

a different hotel. He had to eat his meals alone.

But Robinson loved the game. He played his hardest. He showed that he belonged. He was one of the greatest players of his time.

In the Marathon of Hope, Terry Fox ran 3,339 miles (5,373 km).

In college, basketball player Terry Fox noticed a pain in his leg. It got worse and worse. He went to see a doctor. Tests showed that he had cancer. Doctors had to **amputate** his leg.

Fox's athletic career was in doubt. Still, he did not stop. He worked hard in **physical therapy**. He went through months of cancer treatment. The treatment gave him an idea. He wanted to help others who had cancer.

Fox decided to raise money for cancer **research** by running across Canada. He started in April 1980. He averaged 26 miles (42 km) per day. Many people cheered him on. But his cancer spread to his lungs. After 143 days, he had to stop.

Donations kept pouring in. Fox reached his goal of $24 million by

LET'S DISCUSS

What are some ways to prepare yourself for taking on a challenge?

Fox stopped at his van every few miles for water and rest.

February 1981. He died of cancer a few months later. Since then, the Terry Fox Foundation has raised more than $650 million for cancer research.

Strug was unable to walk on her sprained ankle.

In the 1996 Summer Olympics, the US gymnastics team was depending on Kerri Strug. It was her turn to perform a **vault**. If she scored high enough, the US team would win. But Strug fell and hurt her ankle on her first attempt.

The US team was still in the lead. But Russia could catch up with a good score. That meant Strug had to land her next attempt.

She limped as she began her second vault. Her coach shouted out encouragement. Strug brushed off the injury and started the run. Her bad ankle held as she jumped.

She went twirling in the air. It was a nearly perfect vault.

Strug landed on two feet. But she heard a snap in her ankle. Right away, she pulled up her left foot. Then she lowered herself to the ground. She was in a lot of pain. Strug even had to be carried to the

LET'S DISCUSS

Why do you think Kerri Strug went ahead with her second vault if she was injured?

The US gymnastics team waves to the crowd after winning gold.

medal stand. When she got there, she received her gold medal.

Messi (right) scored a record 73 goals in the 2011–2012 season.

By the time Lionel Messi was 11, he was the best soccer player on the field. But he was also the smallest. Messi had a disease that kept him from growing. He needed treatment. It required him to get a shot every night.

His family could not afford the treatment. So Messi made a hard decision. In 2000, the 13-year-old joined FC Barcelona in Spain. This team could pay for the treatment. But Messi lived in Argentina. He would need to leave his family.

Messi’s courage paid off. With the treatment’s help, he started growing again. He became one of the world’s greatest soccer players.

CHAPTER 3

COURAGE AND YOU

Sports challenge you to be courageous. Every time you compete, there is risk. Sometimes you face a tough opponent. Other times an injury slows you down. Maybe the crowd is against you.

Focusing on a goal helps you to have courage.

All these moments require courage. They require you to be strong and fight through fear.

People face challenges every day. These challenges require courage, even if there's not a gold medal on the line. Maybe it's helping those who are bullied. It could also mean asking for help when you need it.

LET'S DISCUSS

What are some other ways people show courage?

For some people, going to the dentist or doctor can take a lot of courage.

Courage is doing what needs to be done, even if it is hard.

ARE YOU COURAGEOUS?

Ask yourself these questions and decide.

- Do I try to do the right thing?
- Do I do what needs to be done?
- Am I prepared for challenges?
- Do I think positively about challenges?
- Do I notice courage in others?

Courage comes in many forms. Challenge yourself today to do one courageous act. You could sit with someone new at lunch. Or you could ask for help in class.

Something that seems scary or hard might also be fun.

FOCUS ON

COURAGE

Write your answers on a separate piece of paper.

1. Write a sentence that describes how Jackie Robinson showed courage in Chapter 2.
2. Would you move to another country if it meant chasing a dream? Why or why not?
3. How much money did Terry Fox raise by February 1981?
   - A. $3,339
   - B. $24 million
   - C. $650 million
4. What would have happened if Strug had not landed her second vault?
   - A. Russia would have had a chance at gold.
   - B. Strug would have had to try a third vault.
   - C. The US team would have lost right away.

5. What does **obstacles** mean in this book?

*Sports involve many **obstacles**. An athlete's job is to overcome them.*

- A. walls that athletes climb over
- B. different types of sports
- C. challenges that people face

6. What does **field** mean in this book?

*Courage on the **field** can take many forms. It may mean pushing through an injury to finish the job.*

- A. the playing surface of a sport
- B. the list of competitors
- C. a person's career

Answer key on page 32.

GLOSSARY

amputate
To cut off a body part.

discrimination
Unfair treatment of others based on who they are or how they look.

donations
Gifts that people make to help a cause.

insults
Mean comments meant to hurt someone's feelings.

medal
A prize for doing well in a competition.

physical therapy
A process to help a person recover after injury.

research
The act of studying something to learn more about it.

vault
A gymnastics skill that involves leaping and doing turns in the air.

TO LEARN MORE

BOOKS

Herzog, Brad. *Incredible Stories of Courage in Sports*. Minneapolis: Free Spirit Publishing, 2014.

Rice, Dona Herweck. *Physical Feats & Failures*. Huntington Beach, CA: Teacher Created Materials, 2013.

Sundem, Garth. *Real Kids, Real Stories, Real Change: Courageous Actions Around the World*. Minneapolis: Free Spirit Publishing, 2010.

NOTE TO EDUCATORS

Visit **www.focusreaders.com** to find lesson plans, activities, links, and other resources related to this title.

INDEX

Answer Key: 1. Answers will vary; **2.** Answers will vary; **3.** B; **4.** A; **5.** C; **6.** A